A Journey to ELSEWHERE

Poetry Through the Seasons of Life

LEONARD TUCHYNER

Cedar Creek Publishing
Virginia, USA

Leonard Suchynon

To alexis my
favorite neighbor.

This work is dedicated to all those living through the seasons of their lives, and especially to those who have made it into their winter time.

Cover photo by Anna Quillon

Published by
Cedar Creek Publishing
A Virginia Publisher of Virginia Books
Bremo Bluff, VA 23022
www.cedarcreekauthors.com

Printed in the United States of America
Library of Congress Control Number 2014934483
ISBN 978-0-9891465-4-8

TABLE OF CONTENTS

SUMMER

AUTUMN

WINTER

BEYOND

Introduction

Leonard Tuchyner looks back from the perspective of seventy-two years and realizes that life is not a spectator sport. It is filled with beauty, hardship, paradox, joy and suffering, and always there are the options of understanding and growth. Sooner or later, we retire from this life's game, whether we want to or not. The lessons are always about the journey, and the trip is always "A Journey to Elsewhere."

He has tried to capture some of the poetry of this voyage in his book, in the hope that it will help the readers to appreciate the bitter and sweet of their own passages through their present lives.

Many of his insights and experiences have been gleaned from forty-seven years as a psychotherapist in Virginia and Florida, in which people have shared their most intimate experiences–from the profane to the sublime–from the mundane to the spiritual.

A lifetime of gardening, martial arts and love of nature has also been the source of inspiration and understanding. For the last three decades, Mr. Tuchyner has been legally blind, but insists the condition has added to his inner vision.

A GARDENER'S SEASONS

In early Spring the garden grows
with refreshed spirit and vigor,
as new life screams awakening.
The gardener sinks his spade
into dark, moist, rested earth.
Shoots of young life leap joyously
from promising fertile ground.
Fountains of hope flow deep in youth.
There's trust in possibilities.

Summer passion brings competition.
Tomatoes wrestle with weeds and vines,
vying for every glint of sunlight,
thirsting for every drop of moisture,
every inch of nutritive soil.
Until, at last, when summer is spent,
the crackled ground is dry and hard.
Cadaver-sucking, ghoulish vermin
ingest remnants of vitality
from gasping garden vegetables.

The gardener is tired.
His glorious youth is spent.
Fall peeks over his horizon.
But with Fall come reviving winds
that kill sap-sucking parasites.
Now it's time to plant cold-season crops
of kale and other brassica.

Continued

The gardener must find the strength
and will that came so easy when
young blood was clear and hot to spread.
He must nurture a final growth–
one that prefers the chilling cold.
Kale must vanquish remaining moths–
gather sunbeams from waning Sol–
to prosper in that season,
when lush leaves of Spring dry and die,
and bloom to new fruition.

The gardener has one more chance,
while his back and limbs are frail,
to unfold his ultimate bloom
that, in hope, will prepare him for
the dark sleeping night of Winter,
filled with dreams of tomorrow's Spring.

Spring

A NEW SEASON

Time to prepare the garden.
Winter's cold has retreated,
the soil softly thawed.
I know it to be a tease.
Cold winds will blow again,
before gentle spring is sure.
Every year the trickster works
her shifty sleight of hand.
She lures me with her promises
of warm, tender days to come,
and each year I'm fooled by her,
enticed to work the garden.
Trees and daffodils are also snookered–
happy, fortunate delusion.
Buds that swell are better off for it.
They may quiver in the way that buds shiver,
but they survive.
When the warmer, gentler winds arrive,
they gather strength and are equal to the season.
The cherry blossoms will not be delayed.
Though they are delicate in the extreme,
they are much tougher than they seem.
Do not mistake delicacy for frailty.
They will outlast snowfall and wintry wind.
So like the blossoms, I am lured to action,
and my labors are not in vain.

WALKING TO GRAMMAR SCHOOL
IN A DOWNPOUR

Wrapped in melancholy shroud
of late Spring's gentle downpour,
I hear the pitter-patter
of raindrops slapping against
my streaming yellow slicker.
My hands reach deeply into
flapped canvas textured pockets,
sort of dry, yet kind of wet.
I sense my immersion in
bluesy gloomy contentment.

Walking to school, I am secure
in the cloak of my aloneness,
free to be one with spring showers.
My eyes search the grey wet pavement,
as rubber-encased school boy shoes
slosh through shallow splattered puddles,
pacing downpour's droning rhythm,
entranced by mesmerizing drops
off raincoat's hooded dripping brim.

Time is measured in footsteps
counted soft under my breath
lost in the tideless current
of muffled percussion taps.
Somewhere I forget my count,
and time's tide washes away.
In singular universe,
I dwell in its quiet calm.

THE SWINGS AT IRVINGTON PARK, N.J.

"Baby Swinger"

Plumped like a rag doll in a kiddy seat,
as frightened as a flea on fly paper.
This baby seat is too big to snuggle.
I might slip out and fall if I struggle.
My toes are too up to ever touch down.
They must be hanging two miles from the ground.

Papa gives my swing a slow sturdy push.
Earth slips away beneath my dangling limbs.
I clench the safety bar with all my strength,
screech and kick my feet in abject panic.
Daddy is trying to kill me to death.

"Little Big Boy Swinger"

I am a very big boy now,
perched on a narrow wooden slab,
grasping a sturdy metal chain,
I boldly dare to arch way back
and gaze at the cumulus clouds.
Then rotate forward with legs tucked,
and watch the world roll below me.
For I have learned to pump away,
and now I'm a super swinger.

"Almost a Teenager"

Too old to call myself "big boy,"
I ride my sweet swing recklessly,
soaring higher o'er the tree line
to see between its jagged peaks
and glimpse the tiny sailing pond,
a diamond sparkling in sunlight.

I am a bird soaring ever higher
into a clear cerulean bright sky,
then plunging to Earth on a raptor's wings,
rocketing up to the blue sky again.

I'm weight at the end of a pendulum,
until my centrifugal force is spent,
and this floppy tether begins to flap.
I'm lost in a moment of weightlessness.
Heart and breath halt for the chain to snap taut,
when sweet terra comes safely to greet me.

"Old Man"

Someday, as I swing safely
between scenes of life or death,
My restraints will strain and break,
and I will fly unfettered
into the wild blue yonder,
free and wild as every child.

CONEY ISLAND KNISHA MAN,
CIRCA 1947

Three blocks to Coney Island Boardwalk.
Barefooted boys of seven or so.
Tender feet burn on hot white sidewalks,
sizzling blacktop crosswalks.
"Ah, ah, ee, ee, oo, oo. It's hot!"

Under the boardwalk, sands are dirty and cool.
Walk carefully, avoid broken glass.
Bared, sandaled, shooed feet thump,
slide and clack above.
Out of protective shadows into relentless sun,
hot sand, fluffed and tossed by armies of feet.

Umbrellas, blankets, picnic baskets, bathing suits.
Miles-long patchwork of circus colors
on babies, children, young women and old.
Sunning, chatting, reading, sleeping
on carpet-white sand.
In shallow surf, people play
football, beach ball, running and dodging.
Round rubber caps of every shade
bob in the waves.
Rumbling surf, screaming, calling, scolding.
Lifeguard sits high on his tower, bullhorn at side.

Not for us this noon.
The boardwalk waits and beckons,
broad, worn wooden highway.
Watermelon stands, parachute jumps,
bumper cars, steeplechase, Nathan's hotdogs, penny
arcade, and people, people, people.

Vendors pushing carts, one voice is heard.
"Knishes, knishes, the more you buy
the more you want. The more you want,
the more you buy. Knishes."
An old man, with sparse graying hair sings his song.
Our hearts leap. We rush to his side.
Not to buy, but simply to say,
"Hello, Grandpa."

MEAT GRINDING DAY, 1947

A hefty, hard, cast-iron kitchen gear
waited assemblage of detached parts,
on weekly task of meat-grinding day,
to change chop-meat to spaghetti mush,
a proto hamburger or meat loaf.

Clamp it down on the grinding stool.
Feed a chunk of beef. Strain against the crank,
and watch the flesh forced through a holy grill,
tissues squeezed into raw protein stringlets,
a soft striated mass undulating
into a waiting shallow wooden bowl.

Yet this was magic to a youngster's eye,
to watch red lumps drawn by greasy corkscrew
slide into slippery, dark, one-way cave,
from which there was no space for escape.

These days I do not eat flesh,
save for that of finny fish.
And though I cut and feed raw meat
to my domesticated wolves,
it makes my hands feel vile.
I turn to soap and water,
instantly! Really I do.

But straining to turn the crank
and watching the noodled flesh
as they ooze through crushing holes
still holds a strange nostalgia,
like playing with squishy mud
squeezing through my child's fingers.

I guess it's not much different
from the earthy feel of compost,
as I sift it through my bare hands
and find the thoughts of aged manure
are a happy, yummy delight.

WHEN I WAS A BOY, I FLEW A KITE

It was a cool, brisk Autumn day.
Little whirlwinds of fallen leaves
danced their twirling Halloween jigs
up and down sidewalks and the streets,
playful puppies chasing their tails
at my pursuing, skipping feet.

Home from school, under cloud-blown sky,
to my house in afternoon light
and a window two stories high,
High Flyer kite right at my side.

I opened the bedroom window sash,
let out some high-falutin' kite string
and waited for my blue flying thing
to pick up wind and rise on its wing.
I coached it over the lilac bush,
cranked it over telephone wires,
let out two whole new spools of twine
and watched it soar higher and higher.

I fastened the cord to a nail on a board
and closed the window right up tight,
then left the tail-dancing kite to the night.
My folks never noticed,
though it was their bedroom that was hostess.
I dreamt of sails in starlight.
When morning came, I looked near the sunrise.
A darting blue diamond
slipping bravely, darted from side to side
and laughed a hearty "Hi."

LOST WORLD

Where once I knew soft-hilled pastures
and contented, aching moans
of freshened dairy cattle,
my child-sneakered feet slump by
brick-and-mortared, sharp-angled buildings.

I must find my old patch of time,
away from this hard, square newness—
a place I knew that once was real.

Beyond the village walls is a realm—
a field of Autumn grass and bushes—
dried weeds, yellow and stiffly moving
in swirls of olden New Jersey wind.
Skeleton bushes, their bare branches rising,
form sculptures etched in cobalt sky.
A pheasant whizzes on frenzied wings,
disappearing in Autumn brush.
Its chittering ghost sound follows
into this place of long-passed dreams.

An ancient abandoned cottage,
framed by a naked twisted tree,
blends with straw-colored fields.
Its wood-shingled roof strives to protect
this brave rotting fortress, vying against
unstoppable soulless progress.

A cocoon clings to a stalk of broom straw,
one tiny sentinel hoping in the wilderness,
waiting to break out in some distant Spring.

I stride into the meadow land
Into a memory world,
A doomed, lost land
hanging as a picture
on a village apartment wall.

FAITH ON A FRAIL FENCE

This March day, I will mend fence
around my small, humble plot.
I dream of grander spaces
tilled by horse and plow,
but this humble patch
has need for concentration,
a place worthy of my aspirations.
In this simple garden,
my mind and body must bow,
where rows of beets must gather as a crowd.

This fence must protect
against even one grazing thief,
where a single mole can drain its soul,
and dogs that dig
cannot discern carrot from bone.

Alas, this fence is fragile,
made of webbing and bamboo.
A determined mouse could gnaw it through.
This barrier's strength lies only in bluff.
I will gamble on that being enough,
and cultivate my belief in it.
Peas will grow in profusion.
There is need for such illusion.
Life and gardens thrive on hope.

PLANTING SEEDS

There are some who plant the seeds
to watch the green things grow,
to be affirmed in every year
that life, eternally, renews.

There are some who plant the seeds
to eat of Earth's sweet flesh,
to know that they are blessed,
within God's sacred breast.

There are some who plant the seeds
to see the crowns of nature's blooms
sing a song with bumblebees
and drink of holy hues.

But here is one who plants the seeds
to get down on his hands and knees,
touch and smell the loamy soil
and feel and play in muddy toil.

CHRYSALIS

Chrysalis, chrysalis, lying on the ground,
what dark mystic eye decried that you be found?
Praying mantis mother, does she ever pray
for her hundred children, lying in the way?

Wondrous, elegant creature,
with emerald green features,
sits so still, with death its will
preying there on windowsill,
arms folded in watchful peace,
its lover not long deceased.
It seems he did not suit her,
love-bite-beheaded suitor.

Her eighth-inch brood will go,
killing both kin and foe,
murdering each other
like their lethal mother.

With wanting hand of a god,
I reach down to morning sod,
take up this chrysalis nest
of waiting, exquisite death,
and ask for divine pardon
to place it in my garden.

MONKEY MAKER

Pieces here and pieces there,
here and there and everywhere.
Monkey scribbling, stick in sand,
writes the world on which it stands.
Something from nothing is all there is.
Nothing from something monkey can.
Twirling and whirling, castles in the sand,
tide comes and swirls into bands,
bands and bands of wave upon wave,
each one leaves a prize.
A civilization, a book, a rhyme.
A witch, a demon, an angel, a heaven sublime.
Each wave washes away.
Monkey looks to find the maker,
someone to tell him it's all okay.
He leaps and jumps, screams and splashes
shattered waters of sparkling mirror drops.
Each one shows the maker,
a maker with hairy arms and monkey breath.

THE WOVEN WEAVER

The tapestry of life weaves in and out.
The weaver weaves without a bias.
Threads from gold to bitter black,
in and out and out and in,
The fabric turning, spinning about.
A blur of motion, a brownish slur,
flows and slows to stark amazement.
Each thread clear, in turn,
takes surface to dive again
into murky dislocation.
Another strand surfs higher then.
A network of highlights, stark and real,
sharp colors reflect contrasting appeal.
A writhing mass together by love and loathing.
Weaver stands back to watch creation.
How wonderful, how universal, how unique,
how same, how basic.
Weaver falls and falls to tangled disordered,
ordered fabric,
and falls, and falls in love.
Lost in shallows and depths of her creation,
found and lost, lost and found.
She forgets she is the song writer.
Singer becomes the song.
Song and player are as one.
Tapestry weaves and writes the weaver.

EVERYTHING NEW

The first time I saw flowers,
the world was lit with color,
with freshness of early morn,
and the Earth and I were born.

The first time dusky clouds cried,
ground and sky were purified,
so that Earth and I were bathed
in soft melancholy day.

The first time I went sailing,
the sky, wind and water danced.
I was borne along joyous,
on the rhythm of their prance.

The first moment I held her near
my lonely heart found its peer.
Every time I hold her close
it is always still the first.

I would that be my standard,
and the way of all the world,
that each day be a sunrise,
as seen through child-like eyes.

MY FATHER'S WORLD

An old oak table separated us,
a river of solid wrought wood.
I was sixteen. He was forty-two,
survivor of the Great Depression.
My life was peaches and cream.
His father escaped old world pogroms.
They were no threat to me.

My world was open to discovery.
Dad already knew the real and important–
Find a solid world made safe by predictability.
But I sought a world of possibilities.

He feared what could happen.
I feared what might not happen.
He wanted a stone foundation.
I wanted a sailboat flying on the wind.

"You know, Dad, this table is only illusion."
He looked at me, worried and bemused.
"I feel it. I see it. It's real enough for me."

"It has no more substance than space between stars."
He slammed both fists against the wooden top.
My breath caught and my heart stopped.

"There! Is that real enough?"
He shouted with angry cries.

I stared back with shocked, frightened eyes.
He stormed away.
This was not a discussion
for today or any other day.

I envy his simplicity,
the force of will that gave him faith.
But this faith in impression is no faith to me.
He believed in an obvious world.
I try to believe in a world unseen.
And I wonder today, what world he sees.

YEARNING LOTUS BLOSSOM

While dining by a windowed seat,
behind me burned the summer's heat.
I was shielded by the shiny pane,
tended by lovely graceful hands
that rendered my repast enhanced.

Her almond eyes were window bound.
Slow and quiet, with furtive glances,
her arms paused as attention passed,
and in dazzling light her mind danced,
a butterfly enthralled by light
in the sun's scorching passion rites.

She often came my windowed way,
feigning to fill unheeded cups,
though it was clear as glass to notice
it was not on me she was focused,
but on the fevered, ardent day.

What lay beyond that window pane
was passion brighter than Sol's hot flame.
Such wistfulness was unmistaken,
her heart captured and by yearning taken.

Summer

ROADS AND CAREFREE WAYS

Nothing is so quaint and charming
as a small winding country road,
marking borders of garden rows,
defining edge of pasture land.

Meandered paths through woodlands
help us discern forest from trees.
But when trails lose their gentle curves,
their simple quiet solitude,
and byways grow into highways,
they also lose their simple charms.

So here's to the wayward wandering road,
with no particular place to go,
that innocent small town boys wander down
on their way to a secret fishing pond.
May they keep their carefree happy ways
and their wayward innocence forever.

LAZY WIND

Sailboat in a somnolent bay
rocking on sleepy sliding swells,
strings of lacey strewn-out seaweed
slip on sunlit sparkling waters.
Sheets sway on soft salty surges,
slumbering sea-lilts lullaby.

Though sky and air seem unmoving,
bits of flotsam glide slowly by.
Sails hang slack in sun-baked blue sky.
A calm force makes the sailboat ply
across the drowsy mild lagoon,
snuggled in gentle arms of time.

Earth and stars often seem fixed.
Life can slip on in leisure.
Nothing ever seems to change,
but stuff floats by anyway,
and nothing really stays still,
though passage may not be noticed.

Souls rest in eternity's cradle,
in the infinite breath of the sea
of immutable changing ocean.

FINKLESTEIN'S CHRISTMAS TREES

The sound of chains on running board cars.
Snow falling gently on Christmas tree yard.
People haggling on evergreen merits.
A fantastic American Christmas bazaar.

Snow-flecked helpers bind trees to trunks.
Kids in scarves and click tight boots,
bob with hopeful Wonderland eyes,
dance enthralled in winter-capped heads.

Finklestein pulls a tree off the fence.
"Look at this beauty, it's yours for just ten."
"What, are you kidding? It's missing some limbs."
"You've a fine eye for value, it's easy to see.
        Maybe you'll prefer this one over here."

"I'll give you eight, not a dollar more."
"This tree is worth twelve, I'm asking for ten."
"Mary, let's go to another tree yard.
        Messina's trees are better than these."
"Alright, alright, you're a hard man to please.
        Nine and a half. Can't do better than that."
"Nine, you're a thief. Not one penny more."
"Merry Christmas, Sir. It's my gift to you."

Scraggly firs that don't get bought
make fine tepees and forts
for Finkelstein's sons and me.

A BICYCLE JAUNT TO THE CHESAPEAKE

Bicycle ride to Chesapeake,
Ben on his and me on mine,
one hundred long miles to the beach,
time for dad and son to bind.

A full fifty miles each day,
packing tents for campers' stays,
first aid, money and Ben Gay
for black macadam trail ways.

We set out in the early dawn
The sun rose on that cloudless morn
Our spirits jaunty as a fawn
All clear at eighty-five degrees
A beautiful day was decreed.

But blazing Sol had other plans.
Fluid flow at the halfway point
went faster than our mouths could drink.
Blessed are the convenience joints.
Without these places, I do think
we two travelers would have been
sizzling hot puddles of goo
and thickened to a pungent stew.

No need for a steam bath that night.
Our bones soft and our skin well-cooked,
Helios blazed with angry look.

Continued

We hit the tarmac with consternation,
hell-leather-bent with determination.
At ten o'clock, ninety-five in the breeze.
By twelve noon it was one-hundred-and-three.
At two, thermometer threatened to pop
By five o'clock it was over the top.

For the tenth time we were forced to stop,
deeply broiled at the side of the road.
It was jumpin' poppin' hot, hot, hot.

It struck me weird that we stuck in the pot
two idiot people, father and son,
laughing our brains out, beginning to rot,
praying for something to put out the sun.

WHAT GROWS IN MY GARDEN

Ephemeral beet leaves,
root-sprouted rouge rosettes,
red blushing mottled stripes,
fans from soft, fleshy spines,
darkly-deep crimson orbs.
Wilting is too easy.

Ambitious reaching tomato vine,
in dry summer's wilting heat, it dies.
With drink of water it bounds to life.
Its pungent smell is perfume to me.
Small yellow flower attracts the bee,
but spicy scent sets the pests to flee.

Unlikely shapes of the squash family,
butternut, patty pan and zucchini,
acorn, pumpkin, crookneck and spaghetti.
Amazing colors-- brown, creamy yellow,
orange, green, striped. All taste squashy mellow.

Prickly, rough leaves of turnips,
frilly, ferny carrot-tops,
the smooth, silky leaves of chard,
hollow, waxy bell peppers,
fertile, moist, tilthy, black soil.

Spring scallions herald the season.
Take the time to smell the spearmint.
Let the garden sing out to you,
and watch the beanstalks reach the sky.

SUNRISE ON MIAMI SHORE

A small reverent group,
six of us in a troop,
trek through a sandy trail.
Early morning starry sky
and sliver of a moon,
peaceful sea barely speaks
beyond the tidal dune,
our silence held like prayers.

We find a place we can see
ocean gentle waves at play.
We sit down on sandy ground
and wait for the coming day.
Tranquil lappings sing to us.
Still air, fresh with morning dew,
Priestly robe for daylight new.

Shyest stars begin to hide,
sheltering from first pale light.
A deep azure purple hue
heralds our sovereign sun.
Seaward breeze begins to breathe,
kisses our hair and skin.
Crimson color skyward bleeds
and pours across the ocean.

Within suspended time,
Sol breaches briny depths,
exhales a daybreak yawn,
and the world awakens.

Waves start to swell and crash.
Seagulls cry for breakfast.
We are one with sunrise,
as we watch the earth turn
beneath our parent star.

SWIMMING WITH MOON FLOWERS

Delicate pale white moon flowers,
morning glories of the night,
unfurl their sheltering shrouds
and bare soft hidden private souls,
to worship their patron goddess.

As do I, standing naked
in softly flowing breeze,
touching me with lover's tease.
Sweet pollen floats and whispers
scented songs on passion's breath.
Candle-light spills out her window
and joins in starlit night bliss.

I plunge into waiting waters.
Surprised laughing splash welcomes me.
I slide through caressing fluids,
anointment in sacred wine.
Body undulates rhythmic dance,
exhales, strokes, kick-glides, lifts my eyes,
hears soft, gurgling sluicing murmurs.
I have become lost in a world
of pollened air, moon and flowers,
candle light and sultry water,
until there is no more of me,
except the state of ecstasy.

WHEREVER THERE WAS MUSIC

Your music always brings you near.
My life's fulfilled in melodies
that spring like fountains from your voice,
and songs that sing from soft blue eyes.
Thus my heart is filled with your love.

Your fingers caress ivory keys,
and my soul remembers old worlds
of warm dark woods and courtly halls,
comforted in piano themes.
My beloved perched on her bench–
serene passion framed in elegance.

Or a fire-warmed chalet, cold winds raging.
Creaks of bending timbers sway in season's strains.
Within, rhythms mingle with laughing flames.
You pour into a moonlight sonata.
My heart rests in fire's blushing embers.

Our spirits glide on lofting tones,
each flowing note a glow of care.
Every chord binds us to our core.
We soar in our sound together.
In rapturous searing sacred love.

Through eons you have always been here.
As ages turned like pages in a book,
you were with me in every chapter.

Continued

I remember always, by your music,
where we find ourselves in dance, entwined
in the endless effusion of time.

BUBBLES IN THE WIND

When we were six I played with her.
Sometimes we cut out dolls of paper.
Many things we did together.
At seven years I moved away.
Audrey and I no longer played.
How she grew I never knew.

Five years later I sat in school.
What class it was I don't recall.
I heard her name one first school day.
"Audrey something" I heard them say.
She approached the teacher's desk.
When I saw her I looked away.
My mind was totally boggled.
My shocked eyes could only goggle.

I had just begun to notice.
Sex for me was hocus-pocus.
There was a strangeness in some girls.
Something deep inside made me squirm.
An embarrassment I'd disguise
from girls like that I'd look aside.
Audrey had become one of them.
I sat silent and tried to hide.
I never ever said hello.

Looking back, I can clearly tell
her new body did not fit well.

Continued

As I was struggling, so was she.
If she saw me I'll never know.
I didn't even say hello.

Our separate paths stayed far apart,
total strangers despite our past,
too embarrassed to reset the stage.
Times I wonder what's become of her.
Lost is my young friend of innocence.
I feel a loneliness and sorrow
that I was too shy to even try
to build a bridge from olden times
and save the possible tomorrows.

Does she ever think of me with whimsy?
A childhood bubble lost in the wind.

Autumn

HOT YOUNG LIFE

Hot young life burning bright
flings itself on rocks of fate.
Invincible undaunted might,
with flesh that tends to break.

Old cold life with caution finds,
can win a bout with time;
But time walks on with wind that snuffs.
Of time, there is never enough.

THE FIRST LEAF

In morning's light, a yellow leaf,
so early in season, lies at my feet.
Its hawthorn shape, a flint spear point.
Spring is fallen, Autumn is nigh.

In lengthening night,
the moon is crescent,
its arms stretched up,
holds Spring's last wine.

Poplars cradle moon glow,
whispering sweet lullabies
of soft cooling breezes.
Newborn breezes will learn to howl.

How sweet the puppy breath,
whose teeth will freeze to ice,
its cold knives cutting deep,
on soft snow of Christmas scene.

WHERE SHADOWS GROW

In a land of shadows,
shadows do not show.

Once upon a time, tennis balls were white.
Eyes that saw blasted them out of sight.
Then it came to pass
that tennis balls turned black,
and slipped through racket mesh,
for shadows cannot bounce back.

Roads lie still; their edges never move.
Cars and trucks and other wheeled things
follow pathways of tar and stone.
I chased them on two wheels,
secure that streets do not lie.
On bright summer days, chased them through
tunnels of trees, did I.
Then side of the road and sight of the cars
melted like ghosts in murky black skies,
swallowed by shadows of black, shifting leaves,
leopard spots and zebra stripes.

Words on paper sundial clear
began to blur and lose their edge,
shadows blurred by cloud-shrouded light.
The words no longer spoke to me.
I felt my way around bumps on a page.
Slowly words began to sing again.
But only slowly did they sing for me.

With each flash of darkness,
that life thundered down,
I zigged and zagged away and around.
There were tools to be learned
and strategies to discern,
and always love to give me a hand.
Denial, despair, acceptance and victory
are the ways of the hero's lair.

Someday, not far, shadows will win,
And I will fade into the shadow of night.
But remember, my friends,
after night comes the day,
so never, ever despair.

A WALK ON THE BLIND SIDE

Mottled shade and sunshine
bathes the tree-lined foot-path,
as my dog and I tread past.
I search for fallen branches,
half seen in my shadow land,
while Barney dog jigs and jags.

Bright sunlight splashes on the open dam.
I hear the rushing sound of lake water
that swirls its escape through a metal drain.
My feet probe for the worn narrow foot-way
or swishes passage through thigh-high grasses,
until we've trekked to the other end.

Barney wanders our course through the woods,
his taut tether steering me on
to a kind neighbor's bordering yard.
A worn ribbon wound around a tree
tells me that my dog has led me well.

On this clear, bright and sunny day,
this street seems a misty shroud to me.
A house on a hill looms toward us,
like a ship on a gloaming sea,
as it sails by me and Barney.

Somewhere, someone mows a lawn.
One cardinal calls to its mate.
Out of a dwelling, barks escape.
A lone car approaches ahead.
The swish, swish of my striding feet,
through the soft, dewy roadside weeds,
whispers a steady walking song,
as world and people ghost along.

Though details and edges are missed,
there is an allure in the clouds
of my impressionistic realm.
It is filled with soft surprises
of what comes wafting out of mist.

CATARACT SURGERY

One week waits before the blade
reaching down to touch my eye
looking through a crystal darkly.
Behold a world shrouded in cloud.

God bless the surgeon's steady hand.
Bless her eyes steady as eagles',
her mind clear with faultless wisdom.
Bless her team of inspiration.

A world of fog still is blessed.
Is it true of a world unseen?
It's not a place I would like to be.

BUCKETS FROM HEAVEN OR SOMEPLACE

"This is quite a gloomy day,
clearly looks like rain," she says.
"Dogs want walking anyway.
No good stalling or talking,
so let's get on our way."

When we start it's not so bad,
kind of dreary, somewhat weary,
with a little note of sad.
Foreboding, just a tad,
but really not nasty bad.

Then just a few light drops,
not a hell of a lot.
I am optimistic
this trek will stay propitious.

The precipitation gets denser,
I am becoming somewhat tenser.
Oh well, I certainly will not melt,
no matter how much water I'm dealt
or how dourly the droplets pelt.
Dorothy and her bucket be damned.

My adorable caring wife
has hightailed it clear out of sight.
Warm-hearted toward my creaky knees,
normally sets a kindly pace,
but now she is running a race.

Continued

So where is she? Where did she go?
A road-runner headed for home.

She's abandoned me to this torrent,
which stings, drenches and torments.
Oh, the sound of rain in the trees,
often favorite music to me,
hounds like a grand band of banshees
scouring everything away–
invasion of an airborne sea.

I've walked on, walked on, through the wind
and walked on through the wretched rain,
here all alone, thanks to my wife.
Though my dog is drenched and splattered,
I'm full of hope and nearly home.

Oh no! I've been merely wrong.
It seems with all this pelting,
I am most sincerely melting.

OMEN FROM MY TOTEM

Beyond my sliding window door,
birds come to feast on seeds du jour,
an outdoor fare I set out there.
They pay with color, song and flair.

Long have I known my connection
with tiny, wistful lonely bird,
who comes to me in reverie
and gazes through my windowed mind,
seeking to be with me inside,
or calling me to come outside?

On a clear early winter brisk,
he came to me in feathered flesh.
He waited on a feeder perch
and did not choose to flinch away.
His eyes were clouded, like my own.

"Little brown bird, why do you wait?"
He stepped upon proffered finger,
and we gently touched nose to beak.
Then, his mission done, took to flight.

Were they his wings, the day before,
that flapped against my startled face?
And, if so, why did he return?
What message did he bring my way?
What was this bird trying to say?

Continued

The ways of omens are cloudy-eyed,
As are dreams and visions held inside.
What does he see, eyes blind as mine?
And how does he flit through tree-etched skies?

SEASONS OF GRASS

My spirit gallops through
smells of new spring grasses.
Sap stretches toward sizzling Sun
to grow, become, explore, discover.
Earth beckons, "Come dance with me
before youth passes."

Old grass turns to hay.
Green turns to toasty brown,
cures in Autumn's sun,
the color of molasses,
past times of reaching,
holds its growth within–
its cozy inviting aroma comforts.

In the cold long winter light
I will make my bed in soft old grasses,
wrapped in wizened skin
to slumber through the night
till another Spring quickens my blood again.

OVER THE FROZEN MOUNTAIN

Early January morning,
huddled on my cycle, cold air whizzes by.
Over the frozen Blue Ridge
to the Shenandoah Valley,
we climb the mountain,
cold steel mount, you and I.

Through the town of Greene we fly,
fire station to our right,
high school to the left.
Our cozy nest falls behind.

Bleak, brown browsing pastures,
Hay mounds scattered about,
gun-metal-gray winter sky
burns coldly into wind-squinted eyes.
Foothills long and rolling
leap into steep mountain skirts,
become switchback twitching snakes,
rising writhing mountain heights.
Winter-frozen barren woods
accept in frigid resignation.
Ancient crooked hillbilly house
taunts my tortured winding path.

Coiling roadway leaps in flight,
to find zenith in its height.
Boulders swathed in brown and green,
in heavy hard stark rocky scenes,
deep fissures, valley, chiseled sky.
It is here Heaven and Earth abide.

Here a doe and baby eat,
alertly calm to watch us peak.
We plunge to baleful frozen vale,
petrified by twisting speed,
leaning with my iron steed.

Bleak open farmland lies in wait,
offers no shelter from a frozen fate.
I long for hearth and fire grate.

ANCIENT LAIR

It is said that old, dead, dry wood burns the best.
Friendly, steady flames swathe shivering bodies
in warm, comforting radiance.
But there are times I relish greenish wood
that covets pockets of living sap
which remain defiant, entrenched
within bastions of tough woody cells.
Hiding in their lairs, they wait,
tortured by the blazing assault.
Until, like cornered tigers,
they explode from their dens
with hissing tongues of searing sparking steam,
seeking sky, then spent, fall back to Earth,
lost among the embers.

I thrill to their crackling cannon booms
that aim to strike and to ignite.
It satisfies something that lives deep
within my civilized persona
sitting enshrouded in domesticated veneer,
peeking out in ancient wonder,
transfixed by this licking, glowing being
that nourishes, warms and protects.
But like the ones with jungle eyes,
there is always something here
waiting to be the wild, untamed striking beast.

SQUIRREL ON THE EDGE

The air below my window
shatters to fragments of barks.
Barney Dog's over the top,
higher pitched than barks can get.
Blood lust has transformed this pet,
gone crazy by frustration.
He cannot leap twenty feet
to baby squirrel on window ledge.
Frightened creature by the edge,
on precipice of life or death,
killer dog one fall away.

How long can he balance there?
Powerless, I hope for him.
Could the wee thing make the jump,
six feet to the storied deck?
There lies safety off the ground.
Suddenly, he's in the air,
a wondrous spring to haven.
I gasp, then sigh in relief.
Brave little plucky creature,
he almost took a tumble,
torn apart by canine teeth.

Then, as though in taunting us,
flies back to the windowsill,
laughing that, "The joke's on you.
Bark your nasty futile whine.
you'll never ever catch me.
I'm much too fast and clever.

Continued

If you think that jump was good,
then you ain't seen nothing yet."

Many a squirrel has thought the same.
There's a reason for few old squirrels
living in my half-acre plot.
That Barney Dog has played with them,
eaten and spit them out again.
Nevertheless, I admire
this little rascally fellow,
a tiny audacious critter.
I hope he'll make it to bigger.

VICTIM OF INNOCENCE

Tiny fledgling jay
sitting on the ground.
The cat is away,
and so is the hound.

Little wag-tail Barney dog,
home from his walk,
stalks the little bluejay bird
searching for a moth.

Little dog, my little dog,
blameless child with deep brown eyes,
what within thy soul doth lie,
heralds death for blue-tipped wings,
unexpecting bright-eyed thing
who never saw you coming.

Young innocent bluejay imp,
hapless body lying limp.
One clawed foot shakes and stutters.
Heart shudders, barely mutters.

Lay him in the garden, Love.
He will die in peace that way.
You can go and check on him
'til this weary day is old,
feel his body growing cold.

One hour later, no bird remains.

Continued

Could he, perhaps, have flown away
to rise again on feathered wings
or slide forth in a reptile's maw?
Had mother come to comfort him?

Angel of mercy or of death,
please listen to my heart's request.
For this creature must I behest,
who graced the clouds in which it flew.
Protect this patch of skyward blue.

Soft furry loving dog
curls at his master's feet.
His eyes are soft and sweet.
His heart knows naught of wrong.

WHISPERS IN THE DARK

On a wispy clouded shrouded night,
a silent breeze brushes me
across my naked neck.

It stalks on stealthy tip-toed feet
from foul and fetid churchyards,
where twisted, crooked shadowed tombs
dance unholy jigs,
and ghoulish figures shimmer-shine,
then to disappear.
A moaning groan is barely heard
in the stillness of the breeze.

What portals be those closet doors,
where fetid humors waft
on wings of humid, hellish winds
that creep beneath unshielding quilt,
which make the rocking chair to creak
and stir so very slightly?

In a clammy, cobwebbed cellar,
it summons skittering, whispering voices
concealed in darkened crook and cranny
or under stairs beneath my feet,
to trip my soul and drain my brain
and wish me a dreadful Halloween.

Winter

GOING WITH THE FLOW–OR NOT

When I was a young boy
I settled by the sea
and fished off a seawall
which overlooked the banks
of a river's channel
that scoured its way through
the sandy bay bottom.

When tides came they ran with a hustle
and carried schools of west coast mullet.
I and my bare feet with long cane pole
snagged me a daily fish harvest.
When the tide ebbed, it sped like a train,
ten knots, at least, its retreating wane.

With the brazen foolishness of youth
I'd climb down to tooth-sharp rocks below
my dog left barking on the seawall,
launched myself into the rapid flow,
thrilled by the power of the current
as it bore me far out to the Gulf,
my faithful dog chasing on the bank
until there was no bank left at all,
where he sat and waited anxiously.

Now, here is a thing I learned from this–
one of my magnificent follies.
Go with the flow, but not all the way,
lest I be lost in the Gulf's abyss.

I have not strength to fight the torrent;
still there is enough to compromise.
Swim with a gentle unhurried grace
in the direction of my choosing.
Eventually fate will ease its grip.
I'll find myself in gentle waters,
when I might paddle to a safe shore,
where my faithful dog waits evermore
and can collect my catch of the day.

But as years go by, I feel the tide
that drags relentlessly out to sea.
The channel's breadth forever spreads.
Each year haven seems further away.
Beyond my reach, it will be one day.
My devoted dog no longer waits.

Now I hear faint crash of waves
on yon coastline far beyond,
where my ebbing tide comes in.

Do I hear a shadow bark?

WHO'S DRIVING?

I had a dream just last night.
An old fashioned car with an old fashioned seat,
no bar to separate one from the other
two men seated, side by side.
One was old and the other young,
and nothing to separate him from me.

The old man in the driver's seat.
Deft gnarled hands steered the old horse,
venerable teamster's hands on the reins.

Journeys grow long, and ancient arms tire.
"Son, do you think you can give me a hand?"
New hands hold as old ones retire,
yet wise hands linger as youth conspires.
Who's really in charge, young or old?
Does it matter? It's only a dream?
Besides, I know, both men were me.

SLOW WITHDRAWAL

When the world and I were young and new,
I stayed awake as long as I could,
excited for what each day would show.
I jumped out of bed raring to go.
All colors were bright with heart-swelling chords.
Sound sang and shouted, chorused and roared.
Everyone had their own vivid voice
that rang in my ears clarion clear.
My body flowed easily with joy,
and, to my mind, the world was a toy.

Now in Autumn the world fades away.
Days grow dim and starless nights opaque.
Your muffled voices grow faint and vague,
and my bell-tuned ears have turned to tin.
My body cannot go as it did.
Quietly, my senses turn within,
as the outside seems to flee from me.
Hard to know if I am in retreat
or whether its speed has got me beat.
In the final end, will I know
whether I or the world left the show?
Many have faded away so slow.

Nevertheless, I feel quite alive.
Perhaps, in a new place I can thrive.
It's a shame, for here there is much to love.
It could be that in the world to come
there will be for us even more fun.

Continued

Just the same, when all is said and done,
it's not up to me or anyone
whether I or Earth is on the run.
There are no options. Thy will be done.

EVENT HORIZONS

I watch the ship go sailing.
Far out to sea it flies,
reaching for horizon,
to disappear from sight.

So many people, lately,
have cruised the oceans of life,
gone beyond my mortal ken,
somewhere else than space and time?

Yet that ship goes sailing on.
For them, the sky's forever.
Waters flow in calm and storm,
and still they seek horizon.

I, too, chase the setting sun.
Others watch me slide away,
as I sail to Everland.
But when is this journey done?

Eternity's a phantom sea.
Ships and men sail a boundless Tao.
Forever is an always now,
a timeless event horizon.

THE PRODUCE STAND

The bright noon Autumn sun
wrestles feisty breezes
of a bracing, windy day
with light jackets and jaunty spirits.

Ten miles to the country produce stand,
Halloween pumpkins shout in orange.
An old farm lady climbs from her van
which shelters her from the cold day's air.

I walk past laden tables
of hard red juicy apples,
sweet onions and those with tears,
mild, deep green, crispy peppers,
red hot burning ones as well,
white potatoes, sweet potatoes,
good old collards and dark Swiss chard,
some jars of raw local honey.

The old woman patiently waits
with a serene smile on her face,
her back stiffened against the wind,
sunlight sparkling off gaudy rings.

She tallies up our horn-of-plenty.
I ask, "How long will your stand still stay open?"
"Until it gets too cold. Not long now."
We exchange paper for Earth's treasure.
and leave, hoping for many seasons
not too cold for the produce lady.

OLD HOUSE

Paint so old it fades to pink
flakes off at a finger's touch.
Huge scales like dandruff fall
from hard, cracked, and ancient wood
that still clings stubbornly, faithfully,
and protects the house within.

Distorted shingles hard and dry
cover a roof that once knew tin.
A roof still protecting, or trying to,
losing its edges in rotting mold.
Yet few are the drops of despoiling water
that seep to seek and destroy within.

Chill winter air finds homage here
in halls and stairway cold as death.
Ancient furniture in graceless piles,
indignant pieces knew better times,
when carved wood spoke of loving hands.
What eyes now see the noble worth?

Yet charmed sash windows lure dancing light.
Straight walls hold their bright blue hues.
Unmarred ceilings stay solid, unbent.
Sunrooms charm the morning sights.
Wooded vistas and green lawn smile.

Gently sloped, linoleumed floors
hide broad hard floorboards,
waiting to be revealed and shined.

Continued

Gentle ghosts demurely hide.
The old woman alas has died.
No family waits to occupy.
Ninety-seven years this house has lived.
Almost a century it's survived.
Please, please, just one more time.

Old house seeks new life.

THE COMMANDER

He's an old man now,
still six feet plus.
Standing on plastic knees,
he walks with steady stride.

No stranger to hostile waters.
He rises to responsibility,
is not reluctant to take command.
He says of that, "I'm a pain in the ass."

He follows the rules,
but not when they make no sense.
He has cried with bowed head,
in feeling the loyalty of his men.

In peacetime still a pain in the ass,
principal to little children,
and the teachers that would guide them–
"The grades where learning is most real."

These days he fights the ravages of stroke.
Whips his blood-starved but still keen mind
to produce words and stories
that manage to shine,
head bowed only in divine humility.

TRIUMPH

This sixty-seven-year Dakota Woman,
tutored to be a teacher for her people,
ravaged by afflictions of society,
overburdened under mountains of depression,
polluted by oceans of alcohol,
broke down under the onslaught of these storms.

She lived on the dead concrete plains of the cities,
where she huddled with the beaten masses,
learned ways of survival under bridges.
Was swallowed by asylums time and again,
which, in sheltered walls,
kept her bruised heart beating.

Somehow, her bleeding soul was never beaten.
Its stubborn ember's glow never defeated,
her open discerning eyes never dulled,
and her fighting spirit never succumbed.

Today she walks with confidence, head held high,
honest humility, ally to her pride.
Friend to many who, in wonder, look toward her
and understand, through her marvelous standard,
the conspicuous validity of hope.

She revels in simple pleasures.
These are now her treasures in life:
a splash of color, an insight,
a story, a poem, a prayer,
an unexpected fresh delight,
the loving hand of her daughter.

Her glowing ember has become
a flowing flame that fills our world
        with light.

SEASON GROWS COLD

Now the leaves begin to fall.
The pumpkin remains on the vine,
the apples are at their season's best.
Their juices burst in song.
Never were apples SO delicious.
Never were they so alive.

I see the world through eyes so clear,
eyes that close to cataracts,
eyes that must close to see.
How strange this season
when my blood is wise.
Blood that sings of love and tears,
love that grows slow and cold with years.

In only a few days the apples crisp
will turn to mush.
The pumpkin will fall and rot off its vine.

That life should rest at its peak,
That apples should go mealy
at the height of delight.
That refreshing Autumn should bring such color.
That the freshening winds should bring
the cold of death.

FALLEN CYPRESS

What is the weight of a snowflake?
Are the small ones less than the great?
Some hover gently to earth,
crystalline parasols in flight.
Others collect in streaks of white,
reflected in porch and streetlight,
all hours of the clear frigid night.

How many snowflakes, big and small,
laid down a blanket two feet tall,
and a glistening filigree
in needle leaves of evergreen,
to bend it down and make it fall?

It was a snowfall of record—
Virginia, two thousand and nine.
My booted feet sank to knee deep,
pearly, dawnish, grey silver sheen.
You fell across my fronted path
and barely kissed the sloping roof,
a gentle, silent, harmless death—
in your arms a summertime nest.

Remember when I planted you?
It was so very long ago.
Only two feet high were you then.
You grew so fast and very tall.
Your three companions stood with you
in the shade of a dogwood tree.

Continued

One died an early death.
One, a little shorter than you,
remains to fill your vacant space.

Your lush long-living verdant bows,
festooned with supple sprays of youth,
alive as ever in your fall.
'Twas ever reaching out to sky
that held the snow which brought you down.
And so it is that life can kill.

But in that gentle passing on,
you managed not to do a harm.
Through space you leave the sun will shine
on redbud, magnolia and oak
that stood beside you many years.

In life's fullness you gave your life,
that we may prosper all the more.
Wouldst that be said of every soul.

ESTATE SALE

Who lived here?
No one seems to know.
Professional scavengers,
they have their role.
Pick the corpse to the bone.
Let nothing go to waste.
Ashes to ashes, dust to dust.
But who lived here?

Shelves of books have stories to tell.
Biographies, all kept well.
Musicians,
Presidents,
Authors,
Actors, actresses,
American classics.
What do they tell of the eyes
that no longer read them?

The house tells me he went first.
A stout walker, too big for her,
hides in the basement.
Who needs it now?

A children's room.
For grandchildren?
Crayons, in unwrinkled boxes,
A shelf of games,
Monopoly, Sorry, Rotzi.
Their boxes good as new.

Continued

How often were they used?
One worn wicker chair,
used by whom?

A woman's bedroom.
Fluffed towels, fresh crisp linens,
Jewelry,
Simple, elegant.
Classic feminine dark wood dressers.
How long did she sleep here alone?

So many questions.
So many clues.
But the house, in its pristine way,
speaks of gentle friends.

Who stood in those clean new shoes?
One pair of slippers,
cushioned and inviting,
so clean,
so soft.

I will stand in those slippers many times.
I will imagine their owner's soles
they once embraced.
Last night I dreamt a soul escaped.

HOLDING HANDS ON THE BOUNDARY

Two old people side by side,
under moon glow twilight sky–
wispy clouds flow ghostly by–
veils the pale princess of night.

Bayou waters ripple moon light.
Past the old pair it barely slides.
Hummock trees cast purple shadows
on gentle shining waterscape.
They make fluid nuanced textures
of darkness and iridescence.

The old couple holds wrinkled hands
on an aged oak stump, near the edge
of a sheltered languid alcove.
A weathered rowboat patiently waits,
its frayed mooring rope unneeded
in the lazy dreamy lagoon.

Their hearts quicken to the echo
of fishes splashing as they breach
primal amniotic fluid,
for a moment in open air.

They draw ever closer together.
These too will breech this dense, lower world.
As the moonscape evening lingers,
a mourning dove croons its soothing song,
bullfrog bellows for life-giving love.

Continued

A chorus of calming cheeping souls
lays a blanket of life
over those who will grow slowly cold.

The shoreline shadows reach far out,
blurring borders of sky and marsh.
But in this moment of one blessed night,
the old ones do not know or care
of the poison snake that slithers
or the mosquito that seeks prey.

Decay's reek is the smell of life
and margins between are unclear.

SLEIGHS AND SNOWY HILLS

There was always a snowy hill to climb,
wood and iron belly-whopper sled dragged behind,
young tender chafed feet that didn't mind
and would last a day of wintry white,
into a winter's frigid night.

Up the slippery slope we'd go,
to slide on slick steel blades,
toward a flat landing far below,
over and over swift smooth glides.

Steal rudders made way for sails.
Rain doesn't freeze in Miami sun.
No longer icy canted banks to ply.
Downwind breezes became my slides,
oars and tacks my uphill tracks,
blistered palms my chafed cold heels.

I returned to home of sometime snows,
and in my late fifties years
some lonely streets held pristine winter falls,
in ways my childhood held dear.
But I was the only one who seemed to climb
with my ancient wooden sled behind.
Three ascents were all my body could abide.

Now snowy slopes are but a memory.
White flake falls are followed by plows,
with scraping and chemical salts.

Continued

And I wonder, would I still walk those steeps
to sail down the bumpy silky white,
or just sit and hear echoes of child laughter
that, on such days, haunt my longing mind?

Beyond

ALZHEIMER'S

A seascape hangs on her bedroom wall,
tho' its painter's hands rest flaccid
on her quilted lap.
No brush have they touched these many years.
The painter's eyes cannot see their work.
They stare not blankly at its wall.
Her mind perceives only dreamscapes.
How can a mind which saw essence and beauty
and hands that transcribed it so clearly,
be brought to such blindness and immobility?
How can eyes which saw the patterns and lines
know nothing of what stands in their way—
not even faces she loved yesterday?

I miss those skillful hands
and the blue eyes that painted the sky.
It would be so nice if she could just say, "Hi."

WHERE HAVE YOU GONE?

Oh, Dear Legs, where has your strength gone?
Remember when you carried me
on fleet Hermian wings,
through gentle grassy meadows
and rock-strewn mountain slopes?

Oh, Knees that knew no pain
and hips of wild gyrations,
like me, have you been forsaken?

Dear Back, you bore the world with supple grace,
carried my powerful shoulders,
which reached skyward, staunch and triumphant.

Eyes, you once pierced murky fogs
of mystery with eagle vision,
in my mind, which gave its fruits
without hoarding or hesitation.
Have these qualities forsaken you,
as they have deserted me?

But take heart, our heart
beyond hearts beats true,
though we struggle through a dark,
narrowing tunnel
which cramps us into a humble, painful bow.
Though we slide into depths
that bring us to our belly,
our daunted spirit yet lives.

Continued

Though the leaves and fruits of life be blown away,
our roots grow ever more deeply
into the Earth of our creation.
And though the winter of this year
chills and stiffens,
Spring will undeniably come anew.

And though we are old, we will be young again

LOST LAKE

Long time ago, we were family-close.
Can you see the old lakeside beach
hidden in an Orange Mountain vale?
It was big enough for a tennis court
and a concrete handball slab.

You played so hard it blistered your feet.
The blood stained the sun-baked pad.
I saw you hurl a ball that ascended so high
it seemed it would never fall back to earth
and would be lost in the open sky,
as were our youthful spirits and hopes.
Thought we'd last forever.

I watch the picture in my mind
and see it fade to white,
a fading image of blinding light.
Where did we go?

I call every few years.
Your long-dead father's voice answers.
It is a lovely voice, but I can't hear you.
You brag how well your new knees work.
Now you can reach the pantry shelf,
with your patched-up baseball arm.
And I hear your ghost vanishing in time,
with our deserting lost lake memory–
where we were children.

Continued

And I can't tell you how sad I feel.
So I smile behind my telephone
and pretend that we are still there.

WHEN THE WIND IS RIGHT

When a wind comes out of the East,
a roaring rumble comes to me,
syncopated clickety-clack
of iron wheels on jointed tracks,
sentimental sound from the past.
Rollercoaster on trellised rails,
all calling me from time gone by.

Sound's effect can be capricious,
can take me even further back
to earlier model train years,
where Lilliputian cattle cars
follow their predetermined paths
all around my cousin's bedroom,
behind the dresser, out the door,
down the hall, to curve back once more.

Wayward wind comes from the North.
I am in Manhattan town,
riding in a trolley car.
Rocking rhythm makes me doze,
as the streetcar plies its way.

Then I'm in a subway train,
speeding through darkened tunnels.
Outside, streaks of lights rush by.
Squeals of wheels thrill my young ears,
as we race around the curves.

Continued

We brake to an easy stop
at dingy concrete stations,
where storybook people are
poised to swarm aboard the cars,
while others seek their escape
to another dimension,
above the grimy caverns.

I still ride those rails at times,
waiting for the metal squeal
with its clickety-clack's slack.
And I leave to climb those stairs,
ascend to another world,
where a new adventure waits.

I wonder if, in that new place,
I'll be haunted by distant sounds
of ghost whistles and clickety clacks,
calling, beguiling, beckoning back.

MOVING DAY

All her stuff boxed and labeled,
one worn bed no longer warmed,
bedroom dresser drawers now solely,
simply, solemnly hers.
The good china and silverware,
things for which he no longer cares,
have served in this house for twenty years,
where dreams were shared and shattered.
They will now be only hers.

U-Haul, empty rented trailer awaits,
doors open, its hungry mouth agape
ready to devour devoted lives together.

Friends and relatives come to pay their respects
to the couple-dom's untimely death
and to cart away their lives' remains,
pallbearers of wedlock's unraveled skeins.
He is not there to attend the funeral.

Painted smiles hide the pall.
"This is what she says she wants.
She has good reason, after all."
They cover the furniture
with a PROTECTIVE shroud.

A small apartment and swimming pool,
community laundry room and gym,
"This is such a lovely place you've found.

Continued

Everything you'll need is all around."
She smiles, surrounded in ordered disarray.
"Yes, I'll be so happy here."

TEN MILES OF ROAD-KILL

Ten miles to the city
six deer still and broken,
dead at the road's edge.
One raccoon and one red fox,
all victims of the night.

Coming home the other way,
one child waits for her mother
who lies in stiffening sleep
across the black-tar river.

GRAVEYARD UNDER THE PEAR TREE

This Bradford pear tree nourishes me,
slender and tall in the early Fall,
its skinny branches no longer drooped,
as when she's laden with heavy fruit.

I sit beneath her supple limbs,
my back against her slender trunk,
and know her vibrant life is strong,
nourished by bodies of my friends,
who lie beneath the rocks I fetched,
to guard their sacred bones and flesh.

April, my brave gentle Shepherd dog,
a kindlier soul there never was,
ready to sacrifice all for love,
helped to look after my little son.
I buried her in her thirteenth year.

Sarah and Bob came to us next,
one spotted, the other brown and black.
They nurtured each other in their time
and stayed with us when Ben went away.
Now they rest together at my feet.

Patient and peaceful, Shady our cat,
no other way for him to be but that,
seemed to have always abided here,
accepting, with love, all of his dogs.
His death came softly on kitten's paws.

There is Buford who lived just two days.
He rests here, beneath the Bradford pear,
next to Other, not really our cat,
and Connie, my tiny parrot bird,
whose grave holds less than a handful of dirt.

Each one a chapter in my life,
a member of my family.
Even in death they nourish me,
beneath the tall Bradford pear tree.

ACKNOWLEDGEMENTS

This book could not have been created without Elizabeth Solomon and her poetry critique group which, through the years, has vetted every piece included in this work.

I also want to give special thanks to poet Sigrid Mirabella for her generous help in organizing this work into a meaningful presentation.

Finally, to Diane, my wife of thirty-four years, without whom nothing at all would ever be accomplished.